When It's All Said and Done

Monica Anthony

When It's All Said and Done

by

Monica Anthony

Copyright © 2022 Monica Anthony

All rights reserved. No part of this book may be reproduced, distributed, or transmitted in any form or by any means, including photocopying, recording, or other electronic or mechanical methods, without the prior written permission of the author or publisher, except for the use of brief quotations in a book review.

ISBN: 978-1-7366387-7-4

Library of Congress Number: 2022904260

Cover design: Sharlean Muhammad

Published by G Publishing, LLC

Edited by Anthony Ambrogio

Printed in the United States of America.

Dedication

This book is Dedicated to my Sons and Daughters of the CLOTH

To all my sons and daughters of the cloth that I have ever mentored, please create for your ministries a life line that will survive 2024.

Develop a team of efficient leaders. Never be satisfied with good when you know you have been called to be great.

This is a season when the church is being called to a place where you must raise the bar and stay in front of the curve.

There are many benefits to succession planning. If you are going to stay on the cutting edge, you must give more attention to improvement through the development of kingdom instruction. Church, as usual, will never foot the bill of kingdom, so understand the importance of being ready.

Love you always,

Mother Monica B. Anthony

Table of Contents

Foreword i

Chapter 1: 2020—The Year to Remember 1

Chapter 2: A Letter to My Sons 11

Chapter 3: The Last Words of My Mother: "Family First" 22

Chapter 4: When the Life of a Mistress Becomes My-Stress 32

Chapter 5: Daddy, I Was Lost without You 41

Chapter 6: Two Brothers but yet a Lonely Girl 51

Chapter 7: Ministry Miscarriages and Malfunctions 57

Chapter 8: Peanuts and Cracker Jacks 64

Chapter 9: When Destiny Fails to Breathe 74

Chapter 10: The Manipulation of Mantles and the Truth about Spiritual Coverings 85

Chapter 11: Relation-Trips to Relation-Ships 95

Chapter 12: The Improper Use of Succession 101

Foreword

Monica B. Anthony is the Founder and CEO of MBA Global Ministries, the Daughter's Circle, and Sons of the Cloth. For over 30 years, she has been an active contributor in the field of taking care of God's people—overseeing them yet not lording over them. She is a no nonsense, direct, down-to-earth nurturing Master Teacher with vast knowledge, for within her flow exceedingly abundant rivers of living water and wisdom.

Her goals consist of empowering, healing, and supporting people from all different walks of life—from God's little ones to the elderly, with the necessary tools to inspire them to reach their highest aspirations.

She is multifaceted. As a General in God's Kingdom, a natural and spiritual Mother, and a strategically skilled Life Coach, she is a firm believer in having order and setting healthy boundaries, especially in the practice of the sowing and reaping principle. "To thine own self be true" is a vital concept for her. Leading by example, she applies that precept to her own life first, knowing that the time, effort, energy, and resources invested in one's self will have a direct impact on the quality of life one experiences now and well into the future. Secondly, implementing this framework in relationships, she knows that giving to others as God leads, from abundance rather than portion, will bring forth a lasting, effective legacy.

Firmly standing on the biblical Scripture of 2 Timothy 2:15 (KJV), "Study to shew thyself approved unto God, a workman that needeth not to be ashamed, rightly dividing the word of truth," she makes great sacrifices in her life to follow Christ. She pours into and equips both her Sons and Daughters for the advancement of God's Kingdom. She is forever stirring her multifaceted God-given gifts, talents, skills, and abilities to feed and minister to God's sheep according to His Word by the leading of His Holy Spirit. Because she is well aware of pleasing God in all that she does, one of her many specialties is to walkin the Spirit of God in holiness and righteousness, integrity and honesty, thereby being a hearer and doer of God's Word.

As a Life Coach, she knows how to strategically apply the vast rivers of knowledge, life skills, and wisdom that she has gained through her years of experience, intertwined with the Gift of Discernment. She possesses a precise listening ear and brings forth accurate and strategic insights to

When It's All Said and Done

assist others in reaching the next levels of their destiny. As a pioneer, trailblazer, and discerner of truth, she has overcome many obstacles in life and in the church setting—such as rejection, deception, and being misunderstood. Learning from the peaks and valleys of her life experiences and those of others, she brings forth in her book powerfully explosive mind-blowing truths from the inner parts. Being wise as a serpent and humble as a dove, seeing a lot and saying nothing until this proper time, Monica B. Anthony unveils and reveals a wealthy plethora of knowledge, wisdom, and inspiration that shall set the captives and prisoners free for thousands of generations to come.

La Tanya D. Hinton
Apostle, CEO and Founder of Raw
Faw International

A Word from My Pastor, Cedric Thomas

During my Years of Growing, I was in the Church but swayed away. God bought me back to remind me that He will always be there. I love the Lord and thank God for always keeping me. Through the rough seasons of life, I can say I've grown spiritually, mentally, and physically, and I have remained humble through everything, even adversity. May serving God always be understood properly as a blessing, and, through all our endeavors, may humility always be a friend. Mom, this will be your first book of many, and I'm ready to read them all.

A Word from a Daughter in Ministry, Renai Necole

Apostle Monica, you are constantly with me, as I am grateful to God for you, your ministry, and intercession. The other day I was awakened by the Lord with a conversation about your spiritual prenatal vitamins, which are the nourishment that He provides you in thought, word, and deed for those of us whom you are carrying in your spiritual womb. He was allowing me to know just how strategically considered and prepared the process really is; you are amazingly wonderful in Christ Jesus. I am beyond elated to know and have access to the joy you are. May you always be celebrated. May your children both natural and spiritual always rise to Bless you. ... God's Glory is all over you.

Madam Apostle Monica!!! You are not built to break!! Handcrafted, by God, for the performance of Kingdom, Warrior, Curse Breaker, Priesthood Intercessor, and Spiritual Births—demolishing strongholds, overthrowing ancestral altars, destroying yokes of bondage, and setting captives free, to name just a few!!!! You are indeed fearfully and wonderfully made. I appreciate your spiritual surrogacy. The atmosphere of your sanctuary encourages true covenant relations with Abba Father and Safe Deliveries. God trust you to reproduce Discipleship and to rebirth His Church (Bride). The Kingdom of darkness knows you as fearfully and wonderfully made. For there shall be no abortions, miscarriages, stillbirths, or premature births. May you always be heavenly guarded.

A Word from Brian Anthony

The hate is thick all around us. None of them affect your daily living, and we don't hear the noise. The good thing is you must be doing what God has for you; otherwise, they wouldn't be bumpin' gums about God's plans for you. The thicker it gets, the more elevation He's preparing you for. Let 'em chatter, and keep thanking God for the motivation, chile.

Monica Anthony

A Word from David Johnson

Apostle, *now* is the season for being on your face early in the morning and late at night to get a stronger relationship to release this unadulterated word for possessing power. Nations are waiting to hear this dynamic word that God has concreted within.

Chapter 1: 2020—The Year to Remember

I remember it like it was just yesterday, the pain like a fresh wound reopened—the sweet but sad voice of the nurse when she called, speaking so gently, saying, "Your Mom stopped breathing. She has passed on; will you be coming to the hospital?"

"Yes," I exclaimed, "I'm on my way now."

Despite everything else that was going on—from the pandemic to the brutal 21st-century lynching of George Floyd to major lay-offs while death tolls raged—as I think of it now, I can truly say that this was the first time my Faith was greatly challenged. Nevertheless, in the midst of great darkness a ray of light still burned with the promise of blessing coming my way. Blessings not just for me but for all those who believed that God was ready to not only shift the Church but reveal a new revelation about kingdom.

It was April 24, 2021, when I finally sat down in front of my computer and began to write. Someone may be asking, "What's so significant about that date?" And I explain that April 24 was not just the re-announcement of my brother's heavenly birthday but the day my truth became my reality for me, when I had really reached that place where the title of my first book set in motion my drive to create. It had taken me so long, I realized, to sit down and really settle into my desire to write. Some may say, "You are behind time," but I realized what had to happen first, before I could even go forth. It was the day that ignited my passion to never procrastinate again.

As I look back through the revolving doors of time, I see so much, and for so long realized so little, but the year 2020 will go down in history as a time when the world really woke up. A year when significant people were lost, and a season when we really experienced a global shift. A time when technology was advancing, only to be a great benefit to the exposure of hidden travesties. How hurtful a time for parents that were losing their children to the senseless violence of racism that was still prevalent, as the blood of Abel still cried from the ground. Who would have ever thought that 2021 would be the year we would begin to gain ground from the election of a new President, and from families of lost loved ones who would finally not allow a systemic structure to continue to wash over the importance of rights, justice, and freedom for all.

When It's All Said and Done

It was May 12, 2021, when I began to really dive into this first chapter, realizing it would be now or never to get this message out. I felt I had lived life to the full and come to understand that the completion of this work would finally put me in a place of sacrifice, dedication, and accomplishment as I embarked upon a fulfilling journey that would culminate in the manifestation of a product that was designed to express my reason for being and establish a truth that would change my life forever. Which makes me think of a very vital scripture in Philippians 3:14 that says, "I press on towards the mark of even a more higher calling in God through Christ Jesus"—like a gold medal bestowed upon the neck of one in an Earthly race who's arrival to the finish line was astonishingly awesome.

Shockingly though, 2021 was still producing concerns with issues and circumstances that would keep us branded for life. We will never forget this era of great error in a time we never knew would exist—every day facing the terror of a virus and having the cost of life affected now by the pipeline cyberattacks upsetting us all—and the thought of going through the next two years wearing a mask was unbearable.

It's funny how, when you begin to look over your life, you begin to realize that you are about to enter a time when the next ten years could possibly be all she wrote. Which alerts you to the importance of finally investing in yourself. How interesting it is that, for the majority of our lives, we are misused until we decide that enough is enough. For I believe that trust is not gambling but establishing what is true and eliminating every deceitful act or gesture perpetrated by manipulating offenders who come to drain the life out of you with no remorse.

Which brings me to this defining moment in my life where I had to call a spade a spade. Takes me back to my first experience with the church from my humble beginnings at Third Baptist church to my final awareness of religious manipulation. As I think back and reminisce, I remember attending New Wine Christian Center, Sword of the Spirit, Chicagoland Christian Center, Greater Zion Temple MB Church, and Family Christian Center of Indiana. (There are eight different locations, but I don't care to mention three, as the people there were found to be very fraudulent and unworthy to be called believers.)

As I now step out into the water from the shores of my past, I am elated by the lessons of life that hit me like waves, and sometimes debilitating currents, but built me into the stellar woman I am today. I must admit, with no regrets, that I live now in the pureness of my own truth, which I can't help but walk in forever. So be forewarned that the coming

When It's All Said and Done

chapters ahead are my life story being given to you straight with no chaser. For life—through lethal releases of reality that rang out like shots fired in the night—has truly taught me lessons that translated to Blessings that would have never meant as much written from another person's perspective. It was nothing but wakeup call after wakeup call—a wakeup call that urged me to change, I sit here now amazed at the time that has passed, but the realities remain so warm and present. It is the experience in understanding, what it took for me to walk through things. I could no longer be stuck, but finally emerge and successfully finish this strong.

I guess Philippians 1:6 speaks to my heart more clearly now, in understanding that my confidence must always be in father God, Who, the scriptures declare, began this good work as a great assignment in me, for I am truly assured in every way that even now He will finish the work that only He can perform. That's for somebody reading this book right now. You must face your truth that, no matter where you find yourself at this appointed time, you need to still know that to wake up again only means God is still at work in your life. I came to realize that everything in me from birth to now would be utilized, and even some things have to be thrown out like dirty diapers. As you grow, some things will even become outdated, and other things expired.

Listen, don't be afraid to admit that you will never know it all, but you will know what you know.

Finally, always expect the unexpected, for I can truly say that I learned the importance of never being caught off guard, and how important it was to be adamant about my personal truth because there will always be times in life when you may enrage people, but just know it's your divine revelation, and most of all your supernatural way of living, that stirs the life of those around you. I really know now, when it's all said and done, that I should have been celebrated, never tolerated, for God's hand was always with me. There was nothing more vital than to know God's primary Call for my life, because, when you are in tune to His frequency, surprisingly your tires in life will never go flat. There are so many important facts about your life, with vital details you can't afford to miss.

I pray that this body of work will encourage someone to focus only on the finish line. No longer should you be pressed out of measure or weighed down in despair; although there will be some during the year who won't make it, I am assured by facts that some of you will. Don't allow God's plan for your life to be aborted; if you need to leave some things behind, then do so. I encourage you today to rid your life now of anything incompatible.

When It's All Said and Done

Some would describe it as the need to purge our closets and ask ourselves, "Do the clothes I still wear really reflect who I am?" because sometimes we must reckon with ourselves that it's time we look better. Colossians 3:12-13 says it best: "Put on therefore as the elect of God, holy and beloved, bowels of mercies, kindness, humbleness of mind, meekness, longsuffering, forbearing one another and forgiving one another."

My prayer is that, going forward in this book, you will begin to understand, as I have, that there is nothing more important than my adventure, excitement, joy, victory, power, healing, and miracles in life that are attached to my destiny. I have come to confirm that the power of the tongue is how I speak over my life. I embrace the words in the book of Genesis where it describes dominion in the Greek, which is spelled Kupiapxia, which means power, authority, and control; in other words, you were born to win. God has not only argued your case but has made a way of escape from any situation that has plagued you. As I daily look back over my life, I am thankful that God has brought me here. Even in the midst of what we all have gone through from January 2020 to now, like blood on the door post, God has passed over our lives because we are marked for greatness. When I think of His goodness and all He has done for me, I can just, like the songwriter says, dance, dance, dance all night.

Well, my friend, Jesus' work was clear, concrete, and unmistakable, and so is yours. You have to know that Christ will and has fought for you. Father God will always be found fighting your case. That is the reason I gave my life to Christ in 1983, because Jesus extended extensive training to His Disciples with an impartation of extreme presence from Heaven, a power like no other, that would bond them together forever. It was back then I came into a covenant relationship, and promised to serve Him till I die.

My journey has been very interesting with ups, downs, pitfalls and turn-arounds, but I am here to say I made it through it all. That is why I am now prompted to finally prepare this piece of my life's story for you because, before you can truly impart wisdom into the life of others, you must first walk the sands yourself and leave an imprint and greater impact.

When I look over my life, I feel I have gone from the Church to the couch; in other words, all that I've been through gives me authorization to counsel you. Many people for years never understood my Ministry, and all that I spoke and taught was because I was the first partaker of all God was saying. That is the life of a great Leader you never have others do what you say to do unless you do what they do. The old proverb says, "Don't do as I do; do as I say." Many Leaders live their lives under this old adage and fail to be good examples. Not only should we strive to be examples, but even more to be *ensamples*. For I have come to an age in my life and have learned that an ensample is a pattern or model left to be imitated; thus, I have always tried to leave footprints that make room for blessings, which one could follow closely.

As I prepare to close out this chapter, I am over joyed and excited about the time that I will be spending with you here. What I can say to those who are preparing to write their own book is, "Get ready, get set, get prepared." Please know that writing your memoir will be a huge task, but it will also be worth all the pain. I must admit it has taken me a long time to start my journey, and, even now, I'm realizing this is no small feat. For me, though, it will be one of the greatest accomplishments this side of Heaven, so I'm looking forward to the finale. As we are now approaching the end of an old year, and the beginning of the new, I feel just like a pregnant woman ready to give birth. As a matter of fact, I will share with those of you who purchased this book, that you have now stepped into a fertile season where what you are now carrying is finally ready to

Monica Anthony

give birth. Birthing something of your own is very rewarding. May your every dream come true.

Chapter 2: A Letter to My Sons

The Bible says, in Psalm 127:3, "Children are indeed a heritage from the Lord, fruit of the womb, a reward from God, a Blessing, and a Gift." My mind often goes back a lot to the days I raised my sons, and the days I saw my eldest son raise his son—there's nothing like generational succession.

The question remains, though, how are we living? What are we passing down to our children and what are our children picking up from us? I always thought it vitally important how I lived in front of my sons, always keeping in mind that what you put in is what you will get out. As I sit back today to evaluate my journey, I've come to realize many things. No matter how well you think you have lived in front of your children, ask yourself, "Did they pick up anything good, or is there still need for even greater direction and input in their still growing lives?"

I have now come to a place in my life when real realities are staring me in the face. I must say there

Monica Anthony

will be a time in your life like the title of this book when you will declare, "When all is said and done"—a phrase which you will hear me repeat throughout this book because it was this particular season that changed my very life. It helped me digest the difficult reality that life is not, and never will be, perfect. There will not always be a good ending to all things, but you must learn to take the good with the bad, the happy with the sad, and still locate a place in it all where you can be glad. I have come to know that there will not always be a celebrated end, but it's up to you to make the best of it.

Well, sons, I did my best. I wasn't always successful, but I can say that I was always striving for success—giving ninety percent while others only gave ten. After a while you learn that you can do bad all by yourself.

As you each continue on this journey, you too will see the picture more clearly; you will see that what Grandma used to say is true—that "Misery does love company." I am proud to say that I have never been a follower but always knew I was born to lead. I think that's where you both had struggles and tug-of-wars because you were not comfortable with your own company, for some reason. I noticed your uneasiness; in your times of emotional difficulty, you always aligned your life with people and never spent much time alone, you always seemed to just need someone around. I on the other hand made a declaration to myself years ago that, if these people were not good for me, I would remain alone. Thinking back on it now, I see that it works out better in the end when you learn to spend time alone and enjoy the pleasure of investing in yourself.

I think that's the first lesson I would instill in you both, and the second would be finance, finance, finance. Why? Because the year 2020 taught me to stay ready and in position for future periods of financial uncertainty. Many of us were caught 'way off guard when the pandemic hit. My prayer remains this: that all your Grandmother worked for, and all that I surrendered for you both will continue to manifest on our family tree; that great bunches of fruit will no longer be lost or spoiled, but you both will come into the wisdom of your fore parent's knowledge that succession is a must in order to overcome bloodline curses and multiply future stocks of great wealth.

That said, there will always be seasons that you must stay aware of—one being the season of financial defense: a time to head off the next season of uncertainty and set up funds for emergency. Listen, being rich doesn't mean having the ability to spend great amounts of money; being rich means (1) having money available to spend for unexpected expenses, (2) managing your affairs properly, and (3) prioritizing while keeping a close eye on things that can derail you.

To sum it all up, this is what I would suggest: always keep an emergency fund, stay ten toes down, stay five years ahead, stay away from creating debt, and understand the importance of longevity and retirement, both of which will pay great dividends. Why is it that our nationality seems to only have two pennies' worth of knowledge when it comes to the rules of life, let alone the word of God—why is that? because we talk a good game, put on a good show, but never spend real time in relationSHIP with God. Hopefully, you will embrace this chapter that I have dedicated specifically to you, for I see the need now to speak my peace. As I think back over my life, I have always been one to be more concerned about others than I was about myself, and what I had to understand is the hardest reality; it's my time now, but who will see about me?

Third point: I pray you each embrace this. We are living in a time when it seems every man is for himself; II Timothy 3.1-4 says it this way: "In the last days, perilous times will come. Men will be lovers of themselves, lovers of money, proud, blasphemers, slanderers, haughty, lovers of pleasures rather than lovers of God."

When It's All Said and Done

Know that life will not always present glad tidings to you; people will be critical and cunning—mostly those close to you. Beware that you are not manipulated by illegal trespassers who ride your train for free and connect to your future for long-term survival. Don't get caught up in situations that imprison you, for God has called us each to be free and at peace. We never ask to come here; we just get parents assigned to us by God, and the parents we get have never been trained for the job; they have to learn as they go. You both will learn as you travel this road called life that you too will be assigned to children you must raise. That's when you will begin to understand that life can become a one-sided game, and you will feel the blunt trauma of sometimes being left alone. The question is, "Can you survive?"

As I write to you, my mind goes back to two years that were very important to me: 1985 and 2002. I will never forget either, for both were years when God heard my prayer for you, and He so graciously moved, upon my request. Almost everything that I have ever asked God for He gave to me, and the things I didn't get I already know my Father protected me from. Our lives have all been challenging, but, as the song writer said, I'm still here.

Which brings me to the fourth principle I want to leave with you: the thought of Determination, because anything worth having is worth waiting for, and, let me tell you, no one is going to ride up to your front door in a royal carriage and give you anything. You will have to work very hard. Work has now become my last name, but the beautiful thing about hard work is, when it's all said and done, you look back and appreciate that which you have built because you made the commitment and dedication to labor.

You know I am a word person, because I believe that life's messages are like hidden treasure; you must be willing to dig for them.

I always taught you that there are two kinds of people in the world, lenders and taker. So which one are you? See, when you are determined about something you want, it means you have made a firm decision with no resolve or capacity to change it. Determination is when you, Michael, decided you wanted to be a troubleshooter fixing computers and you accomplished the completion of the program and passed your certification. It was something I could see in your eyes, Kre'shaun; even as a child, you always had to do it your way. My sons, what is your intent at this time in your life? What are you bent on doing? What would you say your future has been fixated on? If you can answer that question, then that's what you were born to accomplish.

Listen, there is nothing more vital than knowing who you are, where you come from, and where you are going. I guess what I want you each to know is that you come from what your Grandmother would call "good stock." That means you should always tap into your maximum potential. Never be happy with just being mediocre; you were born for better. You both are the stars in my eyes. When I go back in my mind, I can literally see days when you were babies. As far back as I can remember, as you continued to grow, I always thought about what I wanted for you. I need you to decide, now that you are grown, what you want for yourselves.

Dr. Myles Monroe once said, "The wealthiest soil in the earth is in the cemetery" because it is a place where the unfulfilled gifts still lie, and, if we could go back now and mine those areas, how Blessed we would become! Remember your dreams; pursue them. Don't just make them the object of conversation—*move* on them. When I think back on all I started in my life but didn't finish, it's because I quit and gave up, but what you are experiencing now in the finished product of this very book—one goal I did *not* give up on. An unfinished project is something that's brewing on the inside of you, which I call "unused success." I tell you, today wealth is in you, but it's up to you to cause it to increase for you.

I pray that you will not leave here without seeing the power that rests so heavily upon you, that you will not allow something or someone to cause you to lose sight of your spiritual gifting. After your Grandma passed, I always told you that, by the time the Lord takes me home to Glory, you both together will have a net worth that's worthy. Another area of importance you must attend to is that of expanding your horizon by the purchase of property and the expansion of assets. There comes a time you must make that work for you. You remember, when you were little boys, I used to ask you if you wanted to be on the corner asking for quarters or in a corporate office giving orders of instructions. Now that you are men, that reality is about to expose your destiny.

I can't tell you enough how vital life is, and the truth is you only get one. The key to your future will be to make the best of this one try. Don't allow life to pass you by, because it comes and goes very quickly. Before you know it, it's all said and done. Listen, by the time you reach your finale, you want to have accomplished every goal that you set. Don't allow life to be just a drive-by shooting, nor a hit and run. Plan to acquire wealth, health, and wellbeing. Never take the short route, for the long way is more scenic. Never think of life as hard; it's only as hard as you make it. A wise man once said, "No pain, no gain." Your Grandma would say, "If you don't work, you don't eat." Amy Poehler said, "You can change the world by just being yourself." T. S. Eliot said, "Every moment is a fresh beginning." Walt Disney said, "Whatever you do, do it well." Two unknown authors said, "What you think, you become," so "Aspire to inspire before you expire." I think the last one hits home for me. That we should always aspire to inspire, then go higher before we expire.

It's funny how things pan out in life. It never ends the way you think it should. When I think over my life, I am filled with an array of emotions. One thing I know, and that is that I plan to make some great achievements before I leave this Earth, and so will the both of you. I have always prayed for you, asking God to do exceedingly abundantly above all you each could ask, think, or imagine, so keep trying till you get better results. Never limit yourself. Only the strong will survive. Robert H. Schuller said, "Problems are not stop signs; they are guidelines." Johnny Depp said, "One day, the people that don't believe in you will tell everyone how they met you."

I guess I am warming up now, because when, I really set down to write this piece, I found myself procrastinating and being distracted by things that really have no substance. I believe I will get to the finish line because this work is 'way overdue. I must say in my old age I have had to really push myself, believe in myself, and determine in my heart I will focus now on my priorities. So, then, Michael and Kre'shaun, what great things will you do? What will you influence your children with?

I guess what I'm trying to say is this: a memory is still valuable even after the expiration of a dream; nothing will last forever; even your imperfections can become a Blessing. Make your life an adventure. Turn your clouds into a rainbow. For nothing can compensate for doing things in life the right way. My prayer remains that you both will "change the game, and never let the game change you," in the profound voice of Macklemore.

If you expect to reach the finish line, you must be willing to strive for it, dive for it, and thrive till you arrive. Your determination must turn up, and your dedication must take root. What you practice will finally become what you make a habit. For faith is the substance of things hoped for, the Bible says, and the evidence of things not seen. I know you have heard that scripture before—but, if you haven't, start living by it today so your life can change. Never settle for less, but always be your best. For what you carry is destined to be birthed. Even though life won't always be what you plan, give it all you got. In the inspiring words of Nipsy Hussle, stay ten toes down. Expect emotion when you are trying to pursue something. You will never walk into fulfillment until you conquer what you were born to do. I believe you each have a profound story that only you can tell. Never forget that your mess in life will be your ministry. So finish it. In other words, what was a challenge for you will teach you to teach others. Use wisely the hand that you have been dealt. Never feel some kind of a way. Make good use of all you have left.

I'll end this chapter with Seven strong points:

1. Always stay in position to create something new
2. Never fall back, but step up your game
3. Always have the power to reinvent yourself when need be
4. Stay relevant always
5. Never allow an obstacle to defeat you
6. Success doesn't come for free; you will have to work hard for it
7. Never stop working towards your dreams and goals

Chapter 3: The Last Words of My Mother: "Family First"

As I was awakened this morning, it was as if the importance of the day was staring me right in the face. August 12 (1935)—my Mama's birthday.

I started the day in extreme reminiscence, pulling and sending pictures to friends and family and talking about the legacy she left behind. Took me back to the scripture that became my favorite as it surely expresses my Mom's goals and dreams. As I was growing up, there was one thing I would never forget about my Mother: she was a stickler for keeping her visions, aims, and legacy front and center as she spent years teaching us how to handle business and our financial portfolios. My Mom was operating on the principle of Proverbs 13:22 before she ever read the scripture, and I'm not even sure how many times she opened the book, but she was powerful in the things of God without having a church membership when she worshipped Him.

I always told my Mom she was gifted, and had the Mantle of Healing on her life. I remember certain days as if they were yesterday. When we would pray, my Mom's hands would begin to shake uncontrollably. I always knew she was in tune with the supernatural and that God heard her every request. There were not many things she couldn't accomplish, because, if she said it, it was only shortly that I witnessed it come to pass. I'll never forget combing her hair and feeling this dent in her scalp the day she was told she had cancer, and the tears she shed when my Father left our family for another woman.

Through it all, her faith was never shattered, even though it may have been shaken. There were times I saw her bend, but never did she break. Reminds me of her words. "Baby, we come from good stock," and she proved that to be true.

My Mother loved family, cooking great meals, and helping people get on their feet. She could never leave a person wanting, for, if a person was without, not only would she give them something to eat but would put them in a position to create their own stream of income. I'll never forget how, when I was growing up, my Mom would take me to work with her. That is what made all my convictions strong, from my job to my family to my servanthood in church, for, from her, I really learned how to become a woman. My Mother didn't have an easy life; with an unresponsive husband, she understood that, if she wanted something out of life, she would have to create her own wealth, and she did.

My mind travels back to July 29,1964, the day I was born, and how happy everyone was because a girl had finally been born into the Parker family. Life was difficult for me as I was growing up; I always had to play alone because my brothers were years older than me, but I made the best of it. However, making friends was never difficult for me, for people were always drawn to me. And, on the other hand, I loved being the only girl in the family because it meant that I was spoiled and got the attention I needed from my parents.

I must admit I was very afraid of my Father, who was a strange-sized man, and very coarse in his ways towards us. I can remember nights of family tension, and he was always the one with dysfunctional demeaning issues that stirred trouble in paradise. One thing I refused to embrace (and could not fix or defend) was the cries of my mother's helpless stand in an abusive battle that she endured so her children could have a place called home. Running from place to place, partner to partner, and pillow to pillow was never my Mother's desire.

She was a woman of great standards, I must say so myself, who taught great lessons to those ready to receive them, but her mind remained an unsolved mystery and an unresolved battlefield that tortured her destiny and did great damage to her future. As I grew and matured, I tried to help with her weaknesses, but they were unfortunately never resolved; they kept on growing and increasing, until the roots became permanent, eventually contributing to dementia in her later years. Looking at my Mom and remembering her journey made it hard for me to wrap my mind around having to raise a parent who no longer knew who I was, and didn't know how to pronounce my name. You know, as I now look at the pictures of my parents, it's almost like they never existed. Like I don't have a life, and never had a beginning—with that, I'm empty.

How is it that people can lose a vital segment of their life and never recover from it? This is why we must cherish the bodies we live in, and do them justice. We must take care of them, nurture them, and keep them. As I now reach fifty-plus years, it's vitally important to me to now eat clean. I have declared many times that I will not die until I am 100 years old. I asked Father God to grant me those years, and I will get them—but, in order to see years like that, we must eat right, exercise, and be at peace in mind, body, and soul. I truly believe, if my Mother would have had a closer walk with the Father, she could still be here today, and in her right figurative mind. I also believe the same for my brother, and my Father, for your quality of Life is important if you are going to prevail over the gates of hell.

Let me pause here for a moment to give YAH praise for being a God who answers prayer. There are so many stories I can share, and specific ones will be given throughout this book to show you the Power of God. It's saddening to me to think back to the journey from 2015 to 2020 as I was losing my Mom to this demon called dementia. For those who may have family members going through this same fight, pay attention to your family; don't allow them to be mistreated by these swindlers in the world. My Mom was such a giver that, by the time I realized something was wrong, she was giving to over 21 charities. That just shows you how loving she was, but, by then, she was being taken advantage of because of her loss of memory.

I always ask myself the question, "Who would have ever thought my Mom would have lost her mind? Out of all illnesses she could have acquired, why this one?" When I now turn back the hands of time to capture the pain of that season, I pray that, through this memoir, someone will be uplifted and encouraged. If you presently have a parent who is suffering with dementia or know someone who is, after you read this book, share it with someone else, or, better yet, give them a copy as a gift.

Dementia patients can be very difficult to deal with. The key is to work with them where they are. Enter into their world, and live from their point of view. Give them as much freedom as you can, but never allow them to hurt themselves. Be aware that who they use to be will take over, so don't be shocked at what you see, or what you hear. They will be different people every day, so the object of the game is to play a role that keeps them comfortable. There will be days of happiness and joy, and others of fear and even violence; you just have to know how to keep everything level. The truth of the matter is this: they know something is dead wrong; they just can't put their finger on it, so they fight for fear of what they are losing. You can be a great help by assisting them through the most difficult time in their lives when their brains are literally deteriorating and there is absolutely nothing they can do about it.

If they are still driving, it's important that you get a doctor's referral to see a specialist so you can acquire medical documents to keep them safe; then you will have the task of helping them understand what they are going through and helping them adjust to the new life style that is before them. They will hide things from themselves, forget a lot, and never again register new happenings; this is why you will continue hearing them tell the same story day after day, because, as the doctor helped me to understand, their memory reel has no more tape, so they play the same story in their heads over and over and over again. This is how I began to understand something was wrong with my Mom because she would call me over and over again saying the same thing every day in eight or nine calls, one after the other.

It came to the point when I knew it was time for me to move in with her, or to have her to come with me, so she came to live with me. This journey was so hurtful for me, to see my Mother like that, so that's why I'm warning those reading this book: take better care of yourself today than you did on yesterday. You will need your strength, and time for yourself. Dementia is a seven-stage disease which can last from one to seven years.

Like a recorder, my mind goes back from time to time to capture snap shots of Mom's final days. It was concerning, speaking with the doctors, as they said, "Your Mom will need a procedure to drain water from around her heart."

Hospitalization was the same for my Father as it was for my Mother. We took them into the hospital, not knowing they would never make it home. Neither parent liked the hospital and was serious about getting home, not knowing they would never make it back to the house because Father God had other plans.

It came to me so unexpectedly that *I* was now the parent, and my parents became my children, and I had to now make sure they had all they needed. I responded properly, giving them all the care they needed to the best of my ability. It's so in order how God does things. For He always knows what's next while we're attempting to live on and be happy.

I can remember my Father lying there, smiling, as I spoke with his doctors, making sure they took good care of him while he was there. He said, "I heard you over there taking care of your daddy, and keeping those doctors in check."

I smiled and said, "You know what it is. I'm not playing. They best to take good care of you, and I will make sure of that."

You would have never known that my Father and I were estranged for two years, but when I got the call that he was in the hospital, all our strained issues were resolved because Father God made it that way. Bitterness and anger would in no way be our final days together. It's funny how God's plan always overrules Man's plan. All that we went through never made a difference, because he was the progenitor who created my DNA, and there would be no way I could turn against him then.

The last time I would see my Dad forever was the day I walked into his room and watched him breathing strenuously, trying so hard to catch his breath, wanting to remove the oxygen from his nose. It wasn't two minutes after I left the room that they called a code blue—something I had never before experienced. But I understood that it was the life lesson that would prepare me even for the death of my Mother. I was able to understand death in such a way that it would never catch me off guard again.

I stood there in the doorway like Alice in Wonderland, as if my life flashed before me for the last time, with pictures of my Father. The doctor said, "We have revived him five times already. Should we continue?"

With tears in my eyes, I said, "Do all you can for him until you can't do any more, for, when it's all said and done, I will know we did all we could."

At that moment, he flatlined, and I knew I had to let him go. As they cleaned him up, the doctor told me, "Say everything you need to say to him because the last thing to leave at death is the hearing."

When It's All Said and Done

So I began to tell my Daddy everything that was in my heart, letting him know that he did his best, and I wished that he would now rest from all his worries, and, 30 minutes later, he transitioned to a new place.

How wonderful it would be if we knew what the other side of life looks like. Many times, there are those who have had near-death experiences and are able to get just a glimpse of the after world. I can say I saw it once myself. It was as if my light was going out, but, when it's all said and done, Father God will send help from the sanctuary to uphold and protect you. You will know when it's your time, and when it's time to get busy. We each come to Earth with a divine mission to accomplish, and YAH will let no one get in the way.

Monica Anthony

Chapter 4: When the Life of a Mistress Becomes My-Stress

My mind goes all the way back to 1999, remembering a time I met what I thought was the finest man ever. I'd never before dated a man with skin that light, and its luster was alluring. After I ignored his flirtation week after week for what he said was two years, our romance became an on-the-job crush. Out of the blue it hit me like a mysterious attraction that became fascinating, growing into a powerful seduction that neither of us could control, so powerful that we became lovers, and our affair lasted for over 13 years. Boy, how time flies when you are having fun! Unfortunately, ungodly fun never last.

I remember, when he quietly slipped me his phone number and said, "Call me," I was afraid of being caught in the power of his web. I refused for weeks to give in to my desire to know him better. Until I capitulated to his persuasion. Finally, I issued the invitation, and he accepted.

When It's All Said and Done

I remember the night he came over. It was if we'd always known each other. The more we hung out, the deeper the attraction—so deep that the cares of our world went right out the window. As we began to share our life stories, truth was ignored and covered up, and the relationship caught fire. How in the world I got there, I don't know. But it felt right when I knew it was wrong.

The compatibility was so chemically ripe that we existed in this double life for 13 years, think of that. The beautiful thing is we really never had a conflict or problem, and the love-making was a vibe that never lost its ability to lure us into illegal positions that created a bond we couldn't resist, for the addiction for more was inevitable. It was unavoidable and certain to happen. No matter how he tried to kick this pending sensation, it began to call for more until it was official.

We dated as if no document of Matrimony with his name on it existed. For me, it meant closing my eyes to the truth and trying to make something that belonged to someone else magically mine. It's funny how we lie to ourselves—lie ourselves into believing things that have no validity. Lust will slip up on you and become very complicated, so I will just say this to the Mistress: "Never claim him as yours unless Father God gave him to you. Why do we feel we can just walk into someone's Marriage

Covenant, erase their names, and put ours there? *Not so.* So this should begin to shed light on our darkness. Many times, men do wrong without ever feeling guilty, and then constantly return to their folly with that continued lack of regard.

Thinking back to those days causes me to recall every emotional feeling I experienced then—from hurt to confusion to anger, to shock ending in extreme anxiety. Not only were we playing house, but we conceived two children from this interaction of reckless sex. When I look back, I am hurt because my son hurts. Why? Because he doesn't have his Father. What was I thinking? (Obviously, I was never thinking about the worst of what could come out of this wretched situation.)

Some people say honesty is the best policy; the reason relationships are not successful is because no one is honest now. I'll never forget finding out I was pregnant by him and him not wanting me to have the baby. So I was pressed to abort a child that didn't deserve termination. There is a very profound scripture in James 1:15 that says, "When lust has conceived, it bringeth forth sin, and sin, when it is finished, bringeth forth death." Somebody needs to ruminate upon those words because, when you continue in sin, it is a foul misinterpretation of what you should be about when you say you are a servant of God.

When It's All Said and Done

When I look back over my life, I can see how I was always having to prove my faith because I am a woman. I must admit I was not always obedient. That's why my Ministry was corrected often by the Holy Spirit. Be forewarned: all that you attempt to make happen that is not in Father God's plan won't; all that is destined to happen will. Be careful making decisions outside the will of God; you will have to pray, then pay for what you say.

How is it that reality didn't set in for 13 years, and we continued with this soul tie that, when ended, was like the flip side of the coin? How can a love that seemed so right be so wrong? I'm a firm believer now that nothing lasts forever, and every season runs its course. I ask myself often how could I have gotten caught up in such a triangle that could have cost me my life and sadly has caused my son to live all these years without his Father. I'll never forget the pain and suffering I had to endure when my son's Father said to me, "You will be mad at me, and even hate me after tonight, but I must cut this off." Those words cut so deep, but, as I think of it now, it was only my consequences for trying to prey on another woman's man—and, more than that, her *husband*—when I should have been praying for my own.

It's funny how we know better but fail to do better. To the mistress who will read this memoir: The song writer was correct in saying "there is no future in loving a married man; / if you can't see him when you want, you have to see him when you can." He goes on to say, "If loving you is wrong, I don't want to be right."

I will never forget the two day-late holidays, when he couldn't see me on that day because he had to be with his family nor the secret calls in the night with whispers of "I love you; can't get away tonight." Then it all begins to set in—how imprisoned you have become trying to fight for property that doesn't belong to you.

Makes me go back to 2002, when my son was born. His Father said, "I can come see him, but I can't sign the birth certificate." It's funny, mistresses, my sisters—how we are good enough for sex but not good enough to marry. That's when my truth became my reality. My shame was no longer my shackles because I knew it was time to let go.

There will be many different moments in life when you will have to release somethings you love so much so God can finally give you what you deserve. The reason many of us hold on so long is because we are afraid to walk alone, but God has already designed the plan for us, so just walk in it. There will come a season when you don't know what to do; just trust and believe the Father will bring you

When It's All Said and Done

through. You will not be able to continue in a relation-*slip*, so stop fooling yourself into believing that you can because you can't.

Reminds me of the story of the woman at the well in John 4:16 when Jesus said, "Go, call your husband and come back." The woman exclaimed, "I have no husband," and Jesus went on to say, "You are right when you say you have no husband. The fact is you have had five husbands." The woman said, "Sir, I can see that you are a Prophet.

Please know that you can't hide anything from the Lord, and everything you do outside of his will comes with a consequence, then a cost. The reason I said this again is to warn those who are still playing footsie with the devil and tell them, "You lose." Have you ever been on the losing side? Has Father God had to whip you out of ungodly relationships? Here's the truth of the matter: not only did you get laid, but you got played.

What can you say, and please know, even as I am writing, that I'm feeling the sting that is still fresh after years of stepping out on God. Listen—when Satan gets through using you, he has no problem walking out on you and leaving you high and dry. Know that, when his imps can no longer control your mind, they will pack your bags and show you the door, and the word love that came from their lips was just a ploy to keep you hijacked on a trail that was not real. Think back to the red flags the Lord showed you, even as you continued in sin while Father prophesied.

If only we would ever just trust God and no longer be led by our flesh! I'm sitting here now, shaking my head at how deceived we are when we are trying to make things right at the same time we know in our heart that they are wrong. To the husbands in these situations: don't think you won't experience this blazing fire of correction. I promise you it will hit somewhere in your life when you least expect it. It behooves us to shape up and understand that life is real: what you send out is coming back (just as what you sow in this life you will also reap).

Life at times will really make you shake your head. So much wasted time, some may think, but it's not wasted if we can just follow the path. The Father's object is always to get you where you are going without having to endure being broken by a cold, callous, deceitful, manipulating enemy. God has made you smarter than you seem, so just remember that it's you and you alone who set yourself up for every trick of the enemy when you don't use those smarts.

I'll close out this chapter by saying you will live, and you will learn. Life can sometime teach us some strong lessons, which will either shock us or shake us. I promise you nothing lasts forever.

So, to my sisters who have been played like the second fiddle, receive the correction of this season being handed down to you. Be careful—because the same one who lured you in is the same one who will kick you out. The one you cooked for, cleaned for, bought groceries for, paid bills for, washed clothes for, will be the same one to sell you out. Some of you right now have found yourself in this position, and you're probably about to have an anxiety attack. Only thing I can tell you is, "Been there, done that, wearing the t-shirt, and finally writing the book.

I Pray that sharing my personal testimony will help you not repeat the hard road I took because we each choose our path, and, with every path, there is a payment. Some of us will have to admit that, if we only would have listened to God, we would have been okay. But it won't take the pain away; you will have to live through all you do. While the men in this situation may think they were right, they too will pay for their actions. But don't point fingers! After two years, five years, or 13 years, *you* will pay the piper. In other words, you will bear the consequences of an action or activity that you have at one time enjoyed. When it's said and done, sit down and compose yourself from the angered frustration, and nervous rage of disbelief. Then you will also have to walk through a time of grief, but I promise you, when you come out, you will be like pure gold.

Now repent if this is you, and ask God to help you do better. Listen, obey, for temptation will never ever again sway you after you have experienced the loss of the thing that you loved but that didn't love you.

Chapter 5: Daddy, I Was Lost without You

As I sit here tonight, I was shaken out of a dream, thinking back on my past relation-*slips*. I learned this term from a Pastor, Melvin Williams. When he spoke it, it rang heavily not only in my ear but on my heart.

This chapter will be for all the fathers and all the daddies. You do know there is a difference between them, don't you? For fathers give instructions while daddies offer a bit more hands-on in love—at least, that's my perspective. Some would dare to differ with— even debate—that comment, but let's just say we need them more than they really know.

My mind goes back years, trying to capture just one special moment that I can truly say I had with my Father. Believe it or not, it was the last 40 days of his life. Sad to say, this was the only together moment I could share with him, uninterrupted. No distractions from people who only came to bring drama and division.

Seems as though life was never peaceful in the Parkers' Ponderosa, as my Father would refer to our place of residence. I can remember growing up and there being constant tension in our household till one day the decision had to be made that would hurt our family forever. I wonder if fathers know the vital importance of their presence within the household or whether they think their children really notice. Yes, children care, and they depend on their fathers to also be daddies who can cover them, letting them know everything is secure because of their presence. Daddy, if you can hear me in Heaven, I really need you to know I was lost without you.

Still lost today, at times I find myself trying to figure out and navigate my life all at the same time. Still hitting potholes as I drive down the road of existence and attempt to keep the car that is my life well maintained and in alignment.

I remember vividly my Father saying in a harsh and negative voice, "You're going to be just like your Mother." Other people felt the same way, and I must say it's true that I have inherited certain characteristics from my Mother—the most vital being Wisdom. You know, as I have been going through the revolving doors of yesteryear, I have also been feeling the emotion of all I've been through. Today a scripture came to mind that sent

When It's All Said and Done

me back to 1991, the year I got my divorce from my husband. I began to think of the second man I dated after the divorce. I must say that I've always thought that my choice of men has been selective, but, more importantly, I'm happy to say I've never been an around-the-way girl or an all-around girl, and today I'm still happy that my body is preserved.

In Psalm 35:1-28 the Bible says, "Contend with them, oh Lord; fight against those that fight against me. Take up shield and buckler; arise and come to my aid. Then my soul will rejoice in the Lord and delight in his salvation. Command the deep wells of my soul to be unblocked as I Pray, oh Lord, and break forth in Power. For, Lord, I know you to be a storm that can pursue and overtake all conspiring powers whose wish for me is demotion. May every enemy fight themselves, may their camps be confused. Block the wicked, Father, when they think to afflict me. Convict their wrong doing. Frustrate their plans, disgrace their bad behavior. Ambush them, Lord, with a reverse result. In Jesus' name I pray. Amen. May I forever repent for sins committed, and may others do the same."

This Bible chapter was so consoling to my heart, like an ointment promoting healing as I read through the pages, realizing my wounds were still bleeding in areas I thought were already closed. But, as with a darkened area of new bruises, I had to admit I was still hemorrhaging on the inside, still needed to hear my Father's voice, and feel his helping hands.

Daddy, sometimes I feel so lost without you; I'm longing for direction. Wishing our time together could have been longer. Realizing daily how much I look like you, if you only knew. If only your life could have been better for you. If only your trials could have been easier to bear. If only your burdens could have been lighter. Then I could have really come to know that my Father was also my Daddy, whom I could have honored, and respected. Unfortunately, I looked for love in all the wrong places and all the wrong faces. Every relation-*slip* turned out to be fraudulent, involving dealings with men who were extortionists, criminals, perpetrators, bloodsuckers, profiteers, and emotionally malicious.

When I sit back now and do an inventory, I'm so grateful that YAH Father God was with me, saved me, and shielded me from situations that could have been tragically abusive or in some cases fatal. It went from the loss of my virginity too soon, to a marriage that was forced, to infidelity, to outright disrespect. This is where the Daddy piece comes in. Sorry to say, though, when a son never had a Father, he has no example of a measure of rule, of morals needed to be lived by. Instead, he continues in the deficit of his family and passes on what he thinks to be the right instruction, leaving his daughter open to vulnerable onslaughts that can only rape her dignity. I tell you, when it's all said and done, that's when you begin to realize that nothing lasts forever. Life, like a vapor, can be here today and gone tomorrow.

As I am now approaching the fifth chapter of this book, I must say it has really opened up some tender spots in my heart that still hurt to touch—causing me to rehash the memory of a time of my repeated behavior with a dozen dysfunctional men who had one thing in common: a perverse desire for sex but not for the sacred vow of marriage. In doing a complete inspection of my life, I now have come to terms that, out of twelve men, five were serious relationships, three were friendships, and four I can barely remember—which lets me know they came and went. Looking at each of them on paper is interesting, realizing that a couple of them had no significance whatsoever. Please understand, ladies, relationship and marriage are not just about having a man but being with a man who understands that marriage *is* relationship when you are full grown.

I'm sure that, today, the majority of the men I knew then *still* don't know the true meaning of love. Takes my mind back to one of them, who would never hang up the phone without saying "I love you"—and who, I found out, was the most fraudulent of them all.

Sisters, be careful. I know that some of you are sleeping with the enemy as we speak. The love that some people declare is not always love. Stop being fooled by a criminal whose arrest record you never viewed, because, if he possesses an arrest record, then there is no integrity about him.

Why is it that intuition ministers to us about the thief in the night, but we continue to ignore the Spirit's promptings? When will we accept that he is an extortionist, a profiteer, and a bloodsucker living off the wealth of your land while not adding to your pot but selling wolf tickets that have no value? Always counting on the next date night, meal ticket, event, and prosperous moment that will benefit him and not you. Some of you need to ask yourself, "Who is the women here? Why am I always footing the bill and he investing nothing?"

My Sister Jacqui Wilson once said a man always turns out to be the product of his Mother's input, so—to those of you who have sons—what time are you investing in them? Because what you put in is surly what you will get out. You know, when I look at the flow chart of my relation-*slips*, these are the words that come to mind: Low Self-Esteem, Ego, Perversion, Infidelity, Pride, Insecurity, Anger,

When It's All Said and Done

Verbal Abuse, and Manipulation. Like me, I'm sure you are wondering why you are experiencing the same thing in your life. I tell you, big mama was right when she said, "Don't ignore the red flags, and stop giving in to sex before marriage because you will turn around and find yourself thrown out with the bathwater." It is so important that you value your worth, while adding worth to your value. You are a precious gem created by the hands and mind of God, so you should be treated as such. But, when you don't know your value, you allow yourself to be passed around like a joint from mouth to mouth, infected by the saliva of sin.

In case you didn't know it, every man that you gave the opportunity to release himself in you left a deposit with you, and some left other people in you. As we proceed deeper into the exposed chambers of my unsealed vault, take time to do your own inventory to see how many people are still in you. There will be a time when you, like me, will have to examine yourself.

Well, Daddy, it's 2021, and I am finally writing the next chapters of my life. It took me a long time to finally find myself, but I'm glad to say I made it. It was a long road that could have been shortened by the sharing of your wisdom, but I can say that taking the scenic route, even though it was painful, has made me a better woman.

When I think back to the trials, tests, tribulations, and troubles, I now know they were for my good. Romans 8:28 declares everything that happened was for the good of those who are in a relationship with YAH, and those called according to his purpose. This journey has given me many knocks and bumps, but it can only get better, for I'm declaring over myself that my latter house shall be greater than my former house.

Someone else better catch that hook and begin to prophesy over your life. See, the devil never thought I would sell my soul to YAH because he felt that what he had was addictive enough to hold me hostage for life . . . until I broke free. I give honor and praise to the Holy Spirit for his persistence in keeping me even when I didn't want to be kept. I thank Jesus the Christ for his ultimate sacrifice of giving his body and blood for the remission of my sins. And, Father, thank You for leaving me this school of a masterpiece in Your word, the Bible, that was given me, which taught me strategic methods and wholesome verses that transformed me, according to Psalm 51:10-13, which made me realize I was and still am nothing without You.

As you, the reader, are about to transition into this next chapter, take some time to evaluate where you are in your life right now. To thyself be true. Get not caught up on the temporal things of this world, but

When It's All Said and Done

be yet changed. There is still so much ahead of you to be fulfilled; trust that the vision, which you thought had died, was only being held up for the proper time to be birthed. Know that your womb is ripe with possibility. Many may have left you for dead, but YAH is about to do a revamp, a turnaround, a divine shift, because you offered a recent sacrifice that was finally perfect, good, and acceptable unto the Father. You will now experience a grace like no other; GET READY

Fathers, understand that, when you are in the household, your children have the strength to face the world. They seek the goals, dreams, and aspirations you set as they fulfill destiny because of your motivation. Believing in them is like a schoolmaster who anchors them while guiding as a light whose love reflects determination to complete assignments and fulfill destiny. Real Fathers know the sacrifice, blood, sweat, tears, and comfort needed; they're like a body guard who secures and a role model who mentors. Fathers, know that your children look up to you because you are the one who assures them that they can accomplish everything they try.

Always be true to what God called you to do. Any man can be a father, but it takes a special someone to be a Dad. Dads could never birth a child in the world yet never claim them. Who does that? Who allows their DNA to be duplicated in blood but represents another hood? Somebody will catch that hook in a minute.

How can a child share your dreams? Craig D. Lounsbrough said, "The father who has selflessly poured himself into the life of his children may leave no other monument than that of his children. But as for a life well lived, no other monument is necessary." Listen, you can't be boys doing things wrong. I need every Father reading this book to be men who do things right.

According to Genesis 3:9, Father God called to Adam, "Where art thou?", and I believe he's still calling Fathers today. As I approach the conclusion of this chapter, my Prayer is that every father will come to know his place as a most intricate part of the family unit. No longer will a man go around as if all things are well unless he truly bears a connection with his children. May he do everything in his ability to secure the life of his children. May he learn to support the mother of his children when she is left behind in many situations to bear the brunt of the fractured relationship, attending to all the broken places. May the problems no longer just be her portion; may her spouse or partner, too, see his need to fulfill his responsibility. May Fathers now step up to the plate and be counted.

Chapter 6: Two Brothers but yet a Lonely Girl

My mind has been remembering so much as I am writing this book. It has taken me back to May Street, where we grew up and made lots of friends—friends who turned into family, and we did everything together. There was never a dull moment, and, when my friends hurt, I hurt also. When they were hungry, I fed them; thirsty, I gave them to drink; naked, I clothed them; in prison, and I went to minister to them in hopes they would be saved. That's a short summary of my life from adolescence to adulthood.

Since my brothers were older than me by 10 years, it was hard for me to speak their language. But, even though we didn't speak the same language, it was our responsibility to make sure everyone was well. Our family was sure to be monitored by many because my Father was a police officer. Life for us was strange, and at other times very difficult because my Mom and Dad found it hard to maintain a good rapport, and they were married in document only; the passion of their vows no longer exhibited relevance but could be compared to the dark bloodshed battles of war. When I think of my brothers now, I marvel at how they were as different as night and day. Big Mick was from the streets, while Tony (TP) was who I would describe as the Prince of Bel-Air—now, make that dichotomy make sense.

Sometimes I wonder where it all went wrong. For my brother Big Mick's sake, I wish my parents would have had it together. From their broken childhood, to verbal abusive, to a tragic marriage stained by an extra-marital affair. If parents knew what to do, things would be totally different. The Bible asks, "How can two walk together unless they agree?" (Amos, 3:3). The answer is they can't!

Thinking back to my childhood is really hurtful. There is so much I didn't have—moving from place to place, and living with those who were not my biological blood. But, because I was well taken care of, I am grateful to say that I am not lost like I know some are, and was never violated like I know others were. My Mother was a workaholic, but always stepping up her game; we never went lacking. Momma, if you can hear me today, thank you for all you gave to me in powerful, manners, worth, and value, I know now what you meant when you told me, "You come from good stock."

When It's All Said and Done

It was very hard being a girl and having two brothers. It made me feel very masculine to interact with them, and, looking at myself today, I may have very sensual ways, but some would say I'm still a tomboy. I never really was a "girl's girl," because I had to be strong to make it through this world. Looking at my brothers was sometimes insane, and none of us—even though we were born of the same Mother—were the same. We each had a different look, a different plan, and a different demand. Tony was into basketball, Mickey football, and I, being the youngest, always wanted to be a motivational speaker and minister of the Gospel.

A lot of times, we never really understand the impact our childhood has on our future, and that goes for any of us. All that you are suffering now has some long-time effect on who you become. I'm glad I can stand outside myself and create memories that are conducive to a successful end. I always have to thank my Mother for a job well done, for life at times can serve raw steak. Also, it's important to know that you will win some, you will lose some, but through it all you learn life-time lessons that live on.

Thinking about Mickey often brings back memories of his unending struggles, which were many. Of how my Father failed to direct his ability, and how my Mother's insensitive ways could have played a part in sending him to an early grave. Not to mention his jealousy of the way Tony was celebrated, while he and I were just tolerated. Let us be careful, when raising our children, that some are not overrated.

Funny how life for some comes to an end so soon. Many people, I believe, leave before their time because they find it hard to maintain life. This is why you must determine in your heart how many years your life is valued at. What is your net worth, because, if you love life, then you will make the necessary adjustments to strive for something greater.

Mickey couldn't stomach the fact that our parents truly had a favorite child. He had a problem dealing with this reality and thus became a casualty. I declared I would live till 100; I was determined to do so, and I stand on that still today. Unfortunately, my brother left here with gifts and talents intact, never knowing who he was or what he was capable of doing and ready to pursue.

When I think back, I still have so many questions. In my Mother's case, I truly believe, if she would have been more humble, God would have given her a New Spirit. My Mother's life was so difficult—which only proved to me that, if you believe, you will succeed. This is what our parents taught.

When It's All Said and Done

On a lighter note: everyone used to love spending the night at our house. It has always been the place to be. To this day, if you ask my cousins where they grew up having the most fun, they would declare it was at the Parkers' house; Uncle Bill and Aunt Shirley threw all the parties, with great food, and knew how to keep the family together.

I will never forget our first car, and our first house, which I thought to be a paradise made in heaven. I began to see the goodness of YAH's provision 'way back in 1969. Didn't really know that Lord then, but, as I now reflect, I am blessed. My brothers used to have house parties, but I was always too young to participate. On another note, it's funny how Tony used to talk about how he changed my Pampers, and how he would always be there to see about me. Listen, making vows you can't keep is extremely hurtful. We need to work on making our words stick.

I guess I will never get over how they say blood is thicker than water, but, when the going gets tough, the so-called tough get to going. I believe that the loyalties in family should be the strongest and most important, but life proves over and over again that the strong should engage themselves, not fall away. We are living now in difficult times when people have no staying power. I ask myself often what this world is coming to, then I hear the answers of the people who coined the phrase. The world is coming to an end if we don't pray.

As I close this chapter, I remember my brother Big Mick who transitioned from this life in the year 2000. I will never forget you and always say a prayer for you. Will call your name every day. Missing you like crazy. Remembering all the fun we had. Because of that, I can't be sad. It was time for you to get your wings.

Chapter 7: Ministry Miscarriages and Malfunctions

As my mind travels back to 1984, there are bench marks that journal my life in religion. Church has been some type of experience that was never fulfilling. I spent thirty plus years in a lifestyle that only opened me up to ridicule, pain, criticism, dishonor, and fraudulent mishandling. At the time, I didn't understand that it was never the Lord's desire that I suffer by the hands of manipulating hirelings that I would describe as wolves in sheep clothing. Not only were they all in cahoots, but their mode of operation was the same: downright falsity. I never in my life met so many insecure leaders with such low self-esteem. Leaders who always needed to compete to feel they were in the know (only to reveal that they needed much work). When it came to the miscarriages of the ministry, it was the expulsion of devious spirits with an elementary mentality who hindered the anointed and kept them from surviving independently.

This is what caused true ministry to malfunction, for what we describe as church failed terribly, never remained normal, and behaved totally unsatisfactorily. I was one who would speak the truth at the drop of a hat, without delay, and with good reason. Many people with whom I started my Christian journey are still there fighting through the bias and prejudice of an organization that will in some cases never acknowledge the way, the truth, or real light.

Interesting how, this very moment when I decided to write my book, the Bible would depict this as perilous times, and I'm here to say it's so true, being a time of extreme danger, and high risk. We call it the signs of the times, and I truly must admit these times are extremely different. As I go back to decipher my journey, I'm remined of a reformation I was once a part of, only to find out after time that the leader, though married, was sleeping with another woman of the ministry. I never understood how we could dishonor our Father and never ever fear the act of disobedience but yet continue to call our service "Church."

Going through this initiation allowed me to see it was an inadvertent plan to humiliate me until I quit. Funny how schemes can be created around you, and Father God doesn't leave you unaware but relaxes your intuition to know so that the lesson in the end will be a revelatory blessing.

When It's All Said and Done

To show you how people will walk you right into their trap, the question was asked of me once, "If you had to pick the imperfections of your life, what would they be?" I sat there attempting to realize what they would be, but Father God caused there to be no answer, so it left me in a paralyzed state of no response—which caused the questioners to jump to the conclusion, "She thinks she's perfect." How in the world could I be perfect?—not! Just proof again that others worried about me when I wasn't worried about them. As I look back now, I see clearly the schemes, plots, traps, and roadblocks that were set for my demise.

It is interesting also the level of manipulation used within the house of God. How so-called leaders can use you for financial gain and sway people in their treatment of you. Sending messages throughout regions and territories to shortchange and belittle you. Blackball and even stop you. If you only knew the work people put in to stop my flow, my glow, and my dough. No more time will I give to a noneffective work in a church of people who have no regard for truth. Can you imagine someone would put you up to speak, and yet sit behind you with their [prey-er] partner, the same one they were sleeping with behind their wife's back, praying for your downfall when they're supposed to be a Spiritual Covering. What are they covering when they are nurturing their own selfish spirits of arrogance? What I so love about Father God is He will let you suffer only to lift you up when necessary to understand the lesson he taught through those who plotted against you.

I can remember moving from church to church very often and not being able to lay a sure foundation. No matter where I went, it only proved to be improper when it came to serving the Lord in holiness with sanctification. It was a form of Godliness but not according to accurate knowledge, and my knowledge of the word over and over again challenged those who I came in contact with. I'll never forget the "leaders" who told me to remove the title of Apostle from my name and attempted to use my 501c3 to improperly launder unlawful revenue. The list of infractions goes on and on.

Ministry miscarriages and malfunctions are real and a dishonor before Yah, Father God. They happen often in the church. My experience has been vast because I served under leaders who, I realized, had great misapprehension of the holy sacraments of ministry. I have never believed in Bible debate, but I have differed in knowledge from many of the leaders I've served under, and I believe that the relationship you have with Father God pays off when you are intimately grafted in Him. It was my intimacy that allowed me to experience such weight of covenant and relationship, which opened me up to greater revelation and divine prophecy, understanding that these come by prayer and fasting.

There is something so powerful in Matthew 16:18 when it talks of the gates of hell not being able to prevail. A reader who truly understands that phrase knows that it doesn't mean that no one can come against the power of the church but rather that no one can come against the knowledge of His Word. It was Peter's revelation that the gates of Hell could not prevail against His Word because it's not the truth that makes one free, but the truth one knows that makes one free. Who caught that hook?

All I do now at this point in my life is realize and shake my head to think that, at one time, YAH, Father God, prevents our ability to know temporarily so that we experience the lesson. Which is destined to become the Blessing. Where are you in your church function at this time in your life? Where would you say the church is? Where do you think the church is going? We have been so misled in our understanding of the church. Has the church really provided for us the promises and provisions made?

As I go on an all-out examination of the church since the start of the pandemic of 2020 to the newly expanded of 2021 and 2022 as more variants (namely, omicron) continue to spread, I see that the church more and more is losing its value. I have said many times that by 2024 the church will be nonexistent—something I truly believe because technology is so rapidly changing that leaders will no longer have to worry about facilities and salvation; they will continue to be concerned with Bitcoin and the growing of even larger empires. If you think I'm wrong, let's watch to see. Who would have ever thought that technology would be where it is today? We will soon look up and be able to communicate everything with the flick of the wrist. Can you imagine no more paper statements or coins? Yes, this is the future we are headed to. Someone once said we don't utilize our brain enough, and with that I agree.

As I close this chapter, what do you think life will look like in the next ten years? I'm talking about a mere decade from now. As a futurologist, I will share my thoughts as we elevate and expand through these next five chapters. My prayer is that in this book you will locate worthwhile information that is not just for today but for tomorrow, too (information, as a matter of fact, that will last forever). I know they say nothing last forever, but a book should always be a source of reference that calls back your attention, just like a faithful tool that

When It's All Said and Done

offers guidance through navigation and steers your life properly, resulting in progressive success that can never be denied because its instruction was accurate.

Chapter 8: Peanuts and Cracker Jacks

In the next two chapters you will begin to really feel the trauma of my pain if you haven't already, how my journey was exploited by Nuts and Jacklegs in the church. In chapter seven, I asked a very vital question, which we will start unpacking here in chapter eight. For, in the next 10 years, I promise you we will no longer know the church as we know it now. By then, things will be different for many; for example, social media by then will be well known and easily operated. Since we are socializing so strongly on digital platforms now, I wonder what the privacy act will be? It's funny how I never thought about a pandemic until it showed up and now I am constantly concerned about keeping it from invading my life and the lives of my family. Staying alive has now become the challenge of the day.

Have you ever thought about future climate effects, career changes, job seniority, experimental improvement, or robotic engineering? Think of it in terms similar to African Americans going natural

When It's All Said and Done

with their hair—how women went from perming their hair to using no chemicals at all. This is how our lives are about to change. So life without the antics of the church will be the dawning of a new day.

What do you think will be the next step in the expression of our spiritual desires? If you are really in tune with these times, then you know that the car industry is also about to transition as well. Can you even imagine a car-free city? I declare that, 10 years from now, if possible, vehicles will be electrically operated and no longer use gasoline. Keep in mind that we are now dealing with the mindset of a new group of revolutionary leaders who are leaving the X-generation in their dust but are yet still in need of our generational strength and know-how.

Pay attention, also, to how funerals are being handled, with fewer burials and greater choices of cremation. I so remember the day we had such respect for our loved ones that cremation was a thought of dishonor, but now, like anything else, it won't be just a changing of the guards but a changing of the times.

Let's talk more about the changes of 2029:

Climate effects: When I speak of climate effects, I'm speaking in terms of the carbon-dioxide radiation primarily from the combustion of fossil fuels rising since the start of the industrial revolution. Most of the world's greenhouse-gas radiation come from a relatively small number of countries. You do know that Carbon dioxide (CO_2)—a colorless, odorless, non-poisonous gas formed by combustion of carbon and from the respiration of living organisms—is considered a greenhouse gas. Radiation comes from the release of greenhouse gases and/or their precursors into the atmosphere over a specific area and period of time. Carbon-dioxide radiation is a leak stemming from the burning of fossil fuels and the manufacture of cement; such radiation includes carbon dioxide produced by consumption of solid, liquid, and gas fuels as well as gas flaring.

Gas flaring is the burning of natural gas associated with oil extraction. The practice has persisted from the beginning of oil production, and there are many issues that contribute to its misuse, from economic constraints to lack of political will. This natural resource could be used for some many productive purposes. Some of our most needy countries could utilize this resource.

What I'm getting to is the subject of global warming. The other gas we need to talk about would be methane, for it is 80 times more powerful than carbon dioxide as a warming gas.

If there has ever been a time when greater awareness of this subject has been required, now is surely that time—the time to come to a key understanding of what global warming really is, to understand that it's the pollution of our climate that heavily plays a part even in the disruption and decay of our bodies and our health.

Career Changes: One thing we have learned and seen during this pandemic is how our way of doing business has changed so drastically. We have not only discovered how to make our schedules more flexible but how to save revenue by working from home. CEOs are now researching life in this next normal. While the entrepreneurs continue learning how to strive even when things die. Both are learning the importance of embracing digitalization while reorganizing their supply chain. Listen, fine tuning our daily task is necessary—but how will you navigate through these trying times of fighting a disease that is taking lives by the millions?

I've had to consider so much in the last two years that I sometimes found myself becoming overwhelmed—from feeling buried sometimes beneath the death of my Mother to feeling drowned under learning how to start my life over again, but this time without the woman who bore and raised me. With that, I had to step back, take a breath and consider the bigger picture.

So what would you say is trending now? Whatever it is, it will have to play a substantial role in shaping our future as well as increasing our future economy. What are the trends that are now shifting our future? Our goal now must be long term. There must be a competitive advantage for maintenance, expansion, and awakenings that have the capacity to sharpen our view. I promise you the pace of change is speeding up. If you are staying in tune with all the bitcoin platforms, they are all based on time and speed; even when it comes to entering passcode information, if you can't acquire the speed necessary to sustain your position and identify your authenticity, you will get blocked. It's funny how we learned to shift quickly in the first few months of the pandemic. I believe it was our need to survive that kicked in.

I guess what I'm getting to is you can no longer go through life without a plan. You must educate yourself often. You can't afford for another person to know more than you. You must be up on and skilled in the latest trend. For example, for me, what's trending now, second to technology, is becoming cloud literate. There is so much to be learned when it comes to the curve of knowledge.

When It's All Said and Done

I'll end here by saying stay fluent, stay founded and always flourishing.

Experimental Improvement: Have you ever questioned what restaurants are doing with your food before they hand it to you through the drive-through pick-up window?

I'm sure that most of you reading this chapter are trying to figure how I got here and where I'm going with the content. More than that, how and what does this have to do with the title "Peanuts and Cracker Jacks"? As I have homed in on what is harming our environment in gastric combustion, it would be nice to see some future products that will improve our health and wellbeing. For I am looking forward to future enhancements that will fortify us with more vitamins, minerals, and a longer life span. Have you ever put thought to lab-grown meat? I'm realizing now in my 50-plus years of being here on planet Earth that there is so much we don't think about.

This is the reason this chapter is headed in this direction because, not only do I want to share some of my ups, in other cases I want to share my downs. This chapter is vital because I need this book to be a ready resource that stretches beyond just my life in time. We need more books that you can pick up in Barnes and Noble or in online platforms that will act as informants to enlighten you about things 10 years ahead from now. We need to begin to think beyond not just the box but also the four walls of the church.

I have been saddened for many years with the performance of the church because we fail to represent our Father properly. It's funny that we want the pub and perks that come with the provision of salvation, but we offer nothing to the Father in gratitude for all He has done. We scandalize His name, and forge His signature without authority to function under a title that gives homage to the great I AM.

The question remains: will we get right? Or do we continue this all-out comic buffoonery / horseplay, which includes crude characterization and ludicrous improbable behavior? As the scripture would say, "operating under a form of godliness but not according to accurate knowledge" (II Timothy 3:5). Go ahead and repeat that again; it will help us understand really what shape the church is in.

Robotic Engineering: How much thought have we put into what 2029 will really look like? How much attention do we give to what is on the horizon, or do we even care? Self-service has been making its way into our future for some time now. Don't ignore the hints in movies that introduce us to a life where artificial technology is becoming our reality. We now have camera-based security as well as drone photography, which is the technical ability to send robotic assistance on behalf of a company. Just as the owner of the business can create a virtual tour in real estate, so also can drone estimates be given through drone intelligence.

It was June of 2021 that things around me really began to change. Funny how time flies, and desires excel. I began to realize I'd been in my house 19 years and finally began to think differently, not about my place but about my palace. Life is full of great transitions, but they only come in spurts, I went from a beeping alarm system to the automatic recognition of suspicious activities (which already exists) and advancement with camera-based systems.

The pandemic has even showed us what we are capable to do through computer-based learning. I wonder if schools will one day become a passing fad. Truth of the matter is, one day, there will no longer be schools as we know them. As I continue to take inventory and a new view of the world, I have become stuck on the subject of 2029. When I think about it, we have gone from typewriters to laptops, beepers to cell phones; technology, I must say, is truly reshaping our future at the same time that income, race, and gender are still issues that need urgent attention. Global governance for me is a concern, since the battle between Democrats and Republicans has shifted the ease of liberal democracy, now transforming it into a seven-headed beast battling for power, protocol, and cyber protection.

My prayer is that you are alert enough to catch the topics released in this chapter. Like a baseball batting machine, I'm getting this message to you, and I need you to pass it on.

As I prepare now to proceed to this next chapter, I want to focus on how Destiny fails to breathe. I Corinthians 13:9-12 is very expressive in letting me know that we know in part and we prophesy in part. "But when that which is perfect is come, then that which is in part will be done away with."]

"When I was a child, I spoke as a child, I understood as a child, I thought as a child," Paul says, "but, when I became a man, I put away childish things. For now we may see through a glass darkly: but there will be a day when we will see destiny face to face, and then I will come into a complete knowledge to know." This scripture truly brings closure for me, giving explanation to my spiritual journey.

I have had many questions for so long about why I never experienced triumphs and success in the endeavors I believed were God-sent. Question

When It's All Said and Done

remains even with many of you,—did God say it or did you just do it? Good question, huh?—gives us something to think about. Were you sent or did you just went? I know that would be considered Ebonics to some, but, when I express it this way, I'm sure you get a better picture of the significance of my thoughts.

I must say it took me a long time to understand that where I was in my life is where I was supposed to be because of the decisions I decided to make. Understand that the chances you take will cause the results you make. We have been given the ability to create atmospheres with the breath of power given us through the spiritual transmission of dominion and authority through YAH our Father God. This is why you must not copy the life of another when Father has given you a specific plan for yourself. Until we learn to be the person He has called us to be, He can never fulfill His plan or allow you to succeed. He's looking for you to be who he designed you to be. May you always be an original, never ever a copy.

Chapter 9: When Destiny Fails to Breathe

This morning when I woke up, I knew it was necessary to get out early to take care of the business of the day. As we have once again stepped over into a new year, 2022, I know the need of staying active.

Something phenomenal happened this morning that has never happened before. I just began to pay close attention to how blue the sky was, how barren the trees were, but how simply beautiful the sun was shining. The awakening of the day was so powerful, I began to Thank YAH Father God for the ability to see, and how thankful I was to breathe. Even if I feel life dealt me a strange hand, I am still able to see, and, if I can see, I can be. The motivational speakers of our time would say, "If you can see it, you surely can become it"—so, even though only some of my dreams have come through, there are yet still more I seek and can achieve.

It's funny how long we participate in things that are not real—believing in fantasies that have no validity and steadily walking in a wilderness, finding ourselves lost because of those we follow, who are blind. I'm just realizing now, after thirty-plus years, why my destiny failed to breathe. This is not to blame other people for my incompletions, but to release a truth through my life experiences Praying always that someone will learn, then live. It's vital that we live. Many times in life, we experience so many setbacks that we become addicted to the process of being set up for what they call a comeback. Comebacks are too repetitive, and I'm beginning to see that we live our lives on false dreams.

Sometimes I ask myself why it took me so long to get here. Like the song writer says, "It was just my imagination running away with me." I guess it all boils down to this: What God has for me, it is for me. This is where we must begin to live—in that place where I am who God says I am, and I will do what he has designed for me to do. Do we really understand that our life is by design, and everything that happens because we decide so? Every day is built on the determination that I will do, and, in taking a snapshot of my life, I found that the reason I had to learn so many of my lessons was because I was so very hard headed. I believe that being hard headed makes your journey very long and drawn out because you fail to commit to an obedient life style while finding yourself making excuses for the wrong you do.

When I was growing up, my Father always said, "If you lie, you will steal, and, if you steal, you will lie." Even though they are no longer here, I never forgot the strong teachings of my parents. What we fail to understand in that same tense is we stop our own endeavors from breathing, and allow our dreams to die. Our dreams suffocate because we are always looking for validation in something that was never meant to be approved by another. We are born in the flesh but created through Spirit. That's one thing we can never deny—the existence of a universal power. A Spiritual Father we have never seen, but an unction we always feel. It's a knowing that bears witness to a valid reality that YAH/God is real.

If we could ever catch the revelation, we would not only speed up the time of our success, but keep our vision and goals off of life support. Many of us are still sitting in ICU trying to understand why what we prayed for never showed up or how long we will continue to experience respiratory distress. I realize today I am not alone; there are many that can't seem to catch their breath.

I guess this is what I'm trying to say to you who are reading this book: you have so much to live for if

When It's All Said and Done

you could ever get delivered from people. Stop working so hard on pleasing people and please YAH. It's because of him that we move, breathe, and have our being, so, if you are finding it difficult in your life, then there needs to be a readjustment in you. Sometimes we need to go back to the basics, because the church will take you so far out into the deep that you will find yourself outside of the perimeter of truth and that you have entered into teachings of error. It's time to get your life back, your vision well, and your goals on track. There is so much more to you than meets the eye.

Sometimes life is like a backflow waste pipe. The reality is that waste can get so backed up or severely blocked that you will see it pushed out of the pipe in the wrong direction. I'll never forget the morning I went to take the garbage out only to find human feces frozen on the ground, running down the side of the house. I attempted to think of a way I could get it up, but it was frozen. I was truly elated that it was dead winter; could you imagine if it had been mid-summer?

It's so funny how life is, and the hands we are dealt from time to time. We can never be closed minded; believe me, everything you have ever gone through or will ever go through is for you, and for others. Notice I said "for you" first, and then for others. I say it this way because this is the way it makes sense for me. Everyone's journey is personal, and, if we reckon with ourselves first, we will learn the lessons that are meant solely for us.

As I sit here in my home and think about all the time I have lived here, it's a reminder that we should never be peanuts or cracker jacks—meaning never be deceptive, misleading, fraudulent, or a counterfeit.

I could tell you some stories of what happens when deceitful carpenters jackleg the renovation of a home, just to get it sold quicker. Utilizing strong cosmetics to cover up the flaws. I have always had a problem with the plumbing in my house. Reminds me how, when I was growing up, my mama used to say, "Do it right the first time, and you won't have to do it again."

So many things in life are so similar and can be compared to many situations, so, when destiny fails to breathe, that's when I must realize something's wrong. I must realize there is a blockage in my pipe. Even plumbers themselves hate to deal with a cleanout pipe.

See, understanding our lives and our purpose is crucial; it's like grasping the concept of how plumbing and sewage systems work. When things go wrong in the physical world, what your immediate response should be is evident. And so should it be in the spiritual world. It's a good time to search your heart when things don't turn out right, but remember it's always good to call a professional for your spiritual life, just as you do in your physical life. There is one greater than you, who formed you, blew breath into you, and created for you and eternal blue print.

I tell you, when it's all said and done, we will really begin to comprehend this life, and to understand life helps us know people. It's so enlightening when wisdom matures; that's the time when you recognize why people are the way they are. I think I have come full circle in all things. When I now search my emotions, I find that I now employ a no-nonsense approach when it comes to people. The game of life has become old, and wisdom now stands proxy, guaranteeing me a win over every person and every situation that left me for dead. I have found the answer to life, and that is to put on wisdom like a changeable garment. Removing things that are old only to renew them with the new. How long will we stand in places of unproductiveness when success is forever available, and the sky no longer has a limit? That is finally where I have ended up. Like a marathon runner, I've been on the mark for some time now, thought I was ready, but still have a ways to go.

Monica Anthony

As I think of this new place I now find myself in, life span has become extremely important, and my thoughts of longevity and living to age 100 is my reality. What is so beautiful about this life is, once you have caught on to the formula, like mathematics, you then are given the ability to work out every problem. Once you get deep in your life path, you begin to feel, "If I only knew then what I know now, I could have done so much better," but the truth of the matter is every lesson becomes a blessing because it puts you through a divine pressing. For, after the preparation through pressing, comes the privileges of even greater provision. That's why your accomplishments mean so much. Sometimes we just need to look back and remember how we got over.

Well, the appointment finally came again for the serviceman to check for the blockage in my home's plumbing system. I'll never forget that cold day in January when the lesson of life was revealed through the physical faculty of plumbing.

I realized that plumbing harnesses a precious resource called water, which we need and use for so many things, like health, hygiene, and wellbeing. It is plumbing that makes possible the miracle of clean, convenient water—something we often take for granted. Have you ever thought of why plumbing is so important? Well, if you haven't let me help you. What do you think people experience in third-world countries that have no water? Take a moment and think right now where you sit—and what you would do if you had no water?

This is why there are kitchens and bathrooms in the construction of a house; they both serve a purpose. I had to stop and laugh to myself for a moment because, if you have never experienced a cross-up in your septic system, you are missing the beauty of what God was trying to reveal to me. The key is that plumbing has the ability to deliver sanitary, clean water, while at the same time removing filthy waste water. It's this very point that is vital, because the favor is we have been protected from communicable diseases. Listen carefully: public health was created to save your life. Let that marinate another minute.

As I'm getting closer to the end of this chapter, I'm reminded of my beautiful missionary and students in Kenya at St. Mary's. There is so much I desire to provide for them. For, when you realize how blessed we in America are, it is our responsibility to reach out to the less fortunate. My ministry, from the time I was a little girl, has always been to serve the need of those suffering in the grip of poverty, for seeing them eat always made my life complete, and it still does today.

Monica Anthony

I am a firm believer that your ministry is not for you; it's more for others. I wonder how many times in a day we think about the struggles that people in undeveloped countries go through, and how much we take for granted because where we live is well developed. The truth of the matter is you never really think of another person's struggle until you find yourself battling something you can't defeat. What I need you to Praise YAH for is to consider that we take for granted the things that others in dire need would think of as unimaginable luxuries. I'm sure that, during this pandemic, we each have been without something and now know that a life unprepared is a life in despair.

What would you do today if you had no food and water? It's mind blowing how we seldom give thought to the basic things we need, because we are so used to them being there. I can go deeper. What if there were no grocery stores, health-care facilities, schools, dental offices, optometrists, banks, transportation services, job availability, automobiles, day cares, gas stations, and the list goes on and on. Being in a pandemic will cause you to now construct your life in a way where keeping attention on the important things is now priority. There really needs to be a cure for the world's ills. As we now continue our walk through the plagues of this present generation, we better wake up quickly to the needs of these times when we live.

Not only are we having to deal with reparations, a recession, medical shortages in hospital space/staffing, and an economic downturn, but what about gun violence, crime, and police brutality, just to name a few, I tell you we are going nowhere very fast. Who would have ever thought we would come this far only to have to come to a screeching halt for survival. I suggest you do a quick review of where you and your family now stand, and create for yourselves a financial plan. These are serious times we are now living in, and, if you don't generate a new plan different from the one you're now in, there's a chance you will get wiped out. Many people are moving through this pandemic with no concern in the world; I tell you it's past time for a needed change. If you can't change people, learn to change yourself. Be the change your family needs.

Be not just the example, but, as I have taught all my life for those that really know me, be the ensample—there is a difference. I will define this for you before I move on to the next chapter. An example is a thing characteristic of its kind or illustrating a general rule, whereas an ensample exemplifies and actually shows by example. When you search deeper into those definitions, you will locate great pearls of wisdom—namely, that we must not just talk about it, we must finally be that which we talk about. It's time for my destiny to breathe before it's too late.

Chapter 10: The Manipulation of Mantles and the Truth about Spiritual Coverings

Having a spiritual covering means submitting to the authority of another who is a more seasoned Christian believer—putting one's spiritual life and ministry under the direct supervision of another who is more apt to tap the right ventricle of God and get the goods. People who "get the goods" are people who need no kind of announcement because they are so in tune to God's next move that they live, eat, and breathe the true authentic navigated direction of God.

My journey in ministry was long, but all that I have experienced could never just be described as water under a bridge. Not only does my life have leverage, it has measurement; somebody better catch that hook. Even though I am speaking of things here that happened in my past, my mission—by dispensing knowledge—is to catapult you to your future destination with limited interruptions. In this chapter you will learn that you can serve under people's leadership and still have huge differences.

I Thessalonians 5:12-13 proves that there are those who will serve with you and over you but who are in no way worthy enough to nurture or properly cover you. Many of them have no clue that they are to intercede for you and be the class substitute for Father God.

What many still have not come to understand is that covering others in ministry does not give you authority to abuse, misuse, and confuse, as some have done and still do today.

Did you know that the idea of spiritual life and ministry being validated by another human is really not biblical? This is really a movement that was filtered in through the misunderstanding of the scriptures. I won't argue the point on submission because, throughout the scripture, we find that, according to Romans 13:1, we are to be subject to governing authorities because submitting to one another is respect for the protocol and order of worship. I released a prediction about two years ago that, in this year of 2022, this doctrine on spiritual covering is now dying and will become a thing of the past by 2024.

Romans 14:4 is powerful when it asks, "Who are you to pass judgement on the servant of another? It is before his own master that he stands and falls. And he will be upheld, for the Lord is able to make Him stand." The point I'm making here is that, to really understand the truth of spiritual covering, we must go all the way back to the beginning and understand YAHS' role in the Godhead. All throughout the Old Testament, the Bible gave many examples of what we call types and shadows. If I simplify the term, the Old Testament is a basic symbol (type) of what the New Testament would become (shadow). Which means YAH was, through the dynamics of the word, reconciling the world back to Himself. I need someone to see that word right there in action—how YAH didn't just write it through the dedication of 40 spirit-led men but that He was actually the word in action. In revelation 22:13, He declares, "I am the alpha and the omega, the beginning and the ending," so there is not one part of the book that He does not exemplify. In other words, He is, He was, and is still to come.

Since our world has now made a noticeable shift, we must now elevate our knowledge to a place where we know that anything outside of YAH is considered an authoritarian cult with a Charismatic twist. If we do our homework, we will find that this doctrine was given roots in 1970 and has spread like wildfire. YAH is far from one who utilizes manipulation techniques and intimidation tactics, but, in the church setting, I found that many so-called spiritual coverings used various "treats." if you will, as a reward in order to influence participation and the giving of revenue: members were persuaded to give their life's earnings frivolously with no restrictions or control.

Do you not recognize that the acquiring of great amounts of money is the root of this behavior, and has been implemented by ministry molesters who strip, then rape innocent parishioner of not just their 401K, but pensions and social security? Not to mention that some people, in ignorance, have signed their homes and assets over to a regulation created by men and women who honor YAH with their lips but whose hearts, as the Bible declares are far from Him. (Matthew 15:8)

It's time now to selah, pause, and take a good look. Stop sweeping the truth under a rug. Stop covering your leaders' nakedness and allow them to be exposed for their robbery, for taking advantage of the innocent, and for making promises to crown you with power you're not called upon or equipped to handle. It's time we go back to the drawing board on the doctrine of spiritual covering, and rename it spiritual puppetry.

Why do we continue to shut our mouths when we need to speak? Serving pimps and prostitutes posing as Prophets who only come to pretend, giving us no true authority to perform the divine rights of the church? We have been so deceived, but, going forward, I promise you that this too shall pass. No longer will YAH allow you to hold your peace, for you are moving into a season where you will have to fight even greater battles, so get prepared.

No longer will there be self-acclaimed leaders creating reformations with no divine authorization to function. Many were attempting to cover but yet were found under cover and will soon be unveiled and revealed for their unclean bedside manner. Let's be very clear: spiritual covering is an ideology that has very little connection to the truth of scripture, and how unfortunate it is that we serve a God Who is powerful while we who profess covenant are powerless. It is so vital that we give due diligence to the teaching of the Word because somewhere along the line we have missed the true history of YAH. We must now be careful not to become part of movements that, we find out later, misapply and misconstrue the construct of scripture. Why have the Leaders of Christendom not understood that operating in the capacity to cover means "I protect and I nurture"? Being an apostolic covering takes it even further, as in a covenant. If one really understood covenant and became what they taught, the church would truly be what YAH designed it to be. When you look at the total Christian arena, it is true that many teachings have surely strayed from original meaning. No better time than now for the real Apostles (and even Prophets) to stand up and begin to rectify the wrong.

So what does it mean when my mantle has been manipulated? Can I inherit a mantle? Can I be given a mantle? Or is a mantle transferable? These are very strong questions that I will address so that clarity is solidified. It is vitally important that we no longer live our lives by myths, fables, and sagas. Even though these words mean the same, I've repeated them for emphasis, to stress how important it is that we begin to seriously search for truth. There is so much error out here, which explains why many are out here are sheep without a shepherd.

I'm sure that, when I spoke of the mantle, many of you went immediately to the Prophet Elijah and his protégé Elisha. Let's be very clear: the exchange of the mantle was actually the transfer of prophetic authority, which had to do with a calling that was being passed on. Not like we handle business in the church today by washing a neighbor's hands because they wash our hands. We must truly understand the sacred use of power in the church. This, too, is why I will close out chapter twelve with a study on succession because there must always be a leader next in line to lead the order. (I Kings

19:16). When I take a look at the stats of the church, it is evident that maturity is a major flaw and not a factor among present day church goers.

Do you remember how Elijah confronted king Ahab and even had to reprove Queen Jezebel for the murder of Naboth? How about when Elijah called down fire from heaven and consumed 50 Soldiers? My favorite, of which I'm an advocate for, is when Elijah rebuked King Ahaziah for seeking counsel from false gods (II Kings 1:13-17).

The thread I hope to continue in the writing of this book is to get you to understand the wisdom of the priesthood keys that made Elijah worthy of transferring his power. If you truly know of Elisha's urgency to receive from his teacher, their relationship tells the story of what a true mentor/spiritual leader should be in real time. Elisha was determined to know. He was dedicated to his sacrifice of receiving an impartation from Elijah.

Have you ever been in covenant with spiritual leaders, who then became who they set out to be? Were they qualified to throw their mantle over your shoulders? What type of residue was prevalent in their life? What value would you say they released into your life? If Elisha never availed himself of the lessons of life, he would have never been in position for the double portion. This is why we must always be teachable as well as have leaders who are truly investing in our future. It is said that Elijah and Elisha had spiritual history. It is noteworthy that Elisha spent six years with Elijah before he received his mantle, so what is the monkey business that goes on in the church, when leaders assign you to positions that you are not qualified for? That is not to say you have to study long before being elevated, but you need experience before you can teach one.

It says a lot when you refuse to leave the side of your spiritual leader, and your spiritual leader takes great stock in the teachings he or she imparts to you. I'm reminded of a time when I worked under this hireling posing as an Apostle. What true servant of God sets a trap hoping to degrade, disgrace, and dismantle one they are covering? It's funny how you can work with a reformation of leaders, but all the time all they are planning is to fake kick it with you while not merely using you but bruising you. I still see it as if it were yesterday: we stood in the sanctuary signing certificates for affirmation. My signature was utilized to give credence to a tribe of nomads, while my certificate was left unmarked for future authorization of the games people play.

I hope those people will read this book so they will know this: "You thought you broke me when you really promoted me to a level of great discernment." Every lesson contains an extreme blessing. There

When It's All Said and Done

are times when Father YAH won't even allow you to respond to people's nonsense. Doesn't mean you are naïve. I believe the Father sets us up for experiences that give weight to our foundation. For faith is not faith until it is tested. As I travel back through thought, I am thankful for how he kept me through dangers seen and unseen, and now I know it was for my own good. All things happen for the good of those who love the Lord and those who are called according to his purpose.

I find myself smiling a lot when I think of the traps set that now have lingering consequences that will come back and pay astronomical dividends to their owner. Don't miss that, for what goes around does finally come around to those that send it out. For what a man plants into the lives of others shall show up in his garden for making it happen in someone else's garden. Be it positive or negative, you must pay the piper.

Interesting how people think you are weak, and all the time Father YAH is sustaining you and elevating you in the end. What I had to understand is "no pain, no gain." "No worry, no glory." Faith is not faith until it is tested. After the testing comes the establishment of true proven faith. Many times, I felt as if I should have written this book a long time ago, but what I had to learn is that a person writes when it's the appointed time. I can say now that my journey with the Father has been so refreshing. Knowing that you are one who discerns well and is the recipient of God's plan (Amos 3:7) is another added blessing. Just having the pinions of YAH to protect you is oh so nice.

Make it a practice in your life if you haven't already to stay prayed up. The Bible declares, "He that dwelleth in the secret place of the most high God YAH shall abide under the shadow of the Almighty" (Psalm 91). It's good when you understand you have been approved for a later reward because of a former difficulty. *Whew!*—I felt the power on that word. Remember, life is only what you make it. Take advantage now of the time you have been given; making an impact is vital. As I prepare to move on to the last two chapters, I'm now realizing just what life served me—some bad, some good and truly a lot of ugly—but, as Maya Angelou said (and I say in her voice), "Still I rise."

Chapter 11: Relation-Trips to Relation-Ships

What are your thoughts about relationships? How many of you make it a practice to evaluate your friends and associates? How many of you put up with people who should have left your life a long time ago but are still hanging on? It's funny, but life will conclude with a happy ending as long as you stay selective. Always remember you are the captain that steers your ship. Stop allowing illegal trespassers to be privy to the wealth and abundance that YAH has made you beneficiary of.

Your Father is rich in houses and land and will leave to you an inheritance that won't just bless you but is set to benefit your children's children. When you really begin to catch hold of the vision of life, you come to know that people take up residence in your life for a reason; some come for a season while others are destined to be there for a life time. Even though life for us can be times of tested manipulation, it is those times that qualify you as vested. It's the experiences that bring the best out in us, so—because of all that you have been through—

when you're vested, you graduate to a secured place of understanding, wherein you understand your assignment and why you had to endure such pain. I now know that life is a journey already set but which must actually be lived out.

People come, and people will go, but it's up to the Father to teach us to embrace the real ones—meaning not only heterosexual relationships but friendships. Life is full of a variety of associations that leave an impact on your life and person. We must be careful not to allow people to change us or even allow their negative energy to rub off on us. It is easy to become something you are not ordained to be by closely associating with the wrong people, so safe guarding your mind is key. It's very saddening in life how people will take you for granted, and please know this book is not written in this way to be negative; it's for the importance of awareness and enlightenment.

It's so unfortunate in life that people are so caught up in collecting stones—hear me—that they will miss the true value of a diamond. Somebody better catch that hook. Life will always be a challenge, but remember this: every time they told you you couldn't do it, you did.

I still wonder why we are so hungry for the wrong things when life was created to set us up for unlimited possibilities. When you take a moment to turn back the hands of time, what do you find? Are you able to talk about it? We all at one time or another make mistakes, but, somewhere in our journey, it behooves us to get it right. Understand that every person you have had a connection with left some kind of residue in your life. There is a reputation that comes with the people you allow in your circle.

Ask yourself, "What has each relationship filled my life with, and can I say that what was left has any value in it?" Real relationships are those where people walk in and never walk out—because they are concerned enough to never leave you without. But how concerned are you about your own wellbeing? For there are those whom I describe as a chemical substance—a chemical substance that can touch you and create a reaction that causes great devastation.

You should never allow in your life any people who will damage you, but you should welcome those who come to deepen you. Sometimes we must learn how to travel the roads of life open to good company, making sure to advance from tearing down walls to building stronger bridges.

This is never to insinuate that your life will always be difficult and filled with adversity, but there are set times for celebration and careful evaluation of the company you keep. There will be a time when the sun will melt your ice and paralyze the pain of your past so that your present will be empowered by the pleasure of producing strong purpose. I have always opened my life to people I thought would bring me joy, only to realize that some came with bitterness and envy to destroy. When I sit back now and begin to analyze this bigger picture, I realize that it was the pitfalls of puppetry that destroyed my ministry, and the relation-Trips that had power to make me slip.

If you get what I'm saying, then life for you will never be sunshine without rain, so beware of the people who are there to ride your train but never help you on how you maintain beyond the pain. In situations, there will be times when you won't know who's who or what to do, but I promise you will pull through.

Bad relationships should never be the determining factor of how far you go and how you flow. Not all storms come to disrupt your life; sometimes they come to clear your path. I always felt that people really never understood me, and I'm realizing more and more that many were scared, too. Know that every door that closes is not a curse but could be a blessing, so fight on till you overcome and increase the value of your worth. If you never see it manifest, just keep declaring, "I'm Blessed."

As I am getting closer to the end of this chapter and the conclusion of this book, I'm realizing that writing is no joke, and losing something changes the efficiency of your attention, which goes to show you the importance of completing a task properly.

Just the other day, I lost three vital pages of this book because the WiFi lost connection: when I thought I was saving my content, it didn't save. I couldn't believe it when I looked back that it wasn't there. How painful it was to have to go back and start again after all I shared. I'm hoping I've recovered the essence, even though I know a lot of this has changed because life's words never are the same once said.

To all new authors: always utilize two to three ways to capture your line of thought. That's my first lesson in writing this book—keep a copy in several places; that way, you're safe. That's usually how lessons are made to get you ready for your next season.

Back to relationships. It's interesting how YAH will show you the hands and motives of people. How they play games and pit one person against another. This happens in many relationships; that's why possessing the gift of discernment is vital.

Sometimes I say, "If I knew then what I know now, it would have never happened," but I'm a firm believer that it's already meant to be. We've each been dealt a hand, and we must play it.

My advice is for you to know wisdom in all your interactions, for, in knowing wisdom, you will finally come to understand why you had to endure like a good soldier. Have you ever experienced people who literally tried to control you? How dishonorably they deceitfully belittle you? There will come a time when you will no longer play their games, and they will one day have to follow your lead, all the time revealing their true selves. Many people say you should never go back and relive all that you have been through, but I say looking back just to take a review is beneficial to where you are going. I'll end here by saying may your relation-trips become relationships that afford you knowledge that will excel your growth.

Chapter 12: The Improper Use of Succession

How many churches will admit that their ministry has never planned for succession? There is nothing more important than a ministry that prays together because, it's said, it will truly stay together. I can't say I have ever seen one.

Is there a plan in place for when your Senior Leader retires, your secretary takes a sick leave, or your head deacon is promoted to associate pastor? Are you ready when these scenarios take place and leave a ministry vacancy? When a ministry has efficient man power, unexpected plans won't hinder the function of the whole. The most important function of the church is that the members stay mobile and knowledgeable and operate at a level where the body of believers stays well informed. Reminds me of when I managed a foodservice facility; it was vital that we gave each employee a job description and made sure they all were crossed trained.

When we study the history of the church, it is clear that there are still missing links that were truly written in the scriptures but greatly overlooked. A church should never overlook the principles for establishing a solid foundation, and that is through proper succession. There should always be significant strategic initiatives shared among membership that will in turn teach the importance of team work.

Sometimes the members of one local body should attempt to utilize Leaders that are in-house before looking to those outside the house. Not only will it strengthen the unity in the body, but it will keep us focused on the responsibility given us in Matthew 28:18-20.

What's in the pipeline of your church? Do you even know? Are you ready for the changes ahead? Listen, Good Leadership will always spend time making sure shadowing major positions in the body is taking place, so when it is time for replacement the competence of the new leader and experience will easily catapult them to the place they are made for. Like a Track race we must be in position mentally as well as physically to pass the baton to the next official qualified for the work ahead.

Do we in this century know what succession looks like? Was it implemented in our congregations? If you had to explain to a new group of converts in your church how would you describe succession?

When It's All Said and Done

What would you say has been the stand and posture of the church? To understand true succession is to know we must humble ourselves under the mighty hand of God (according to I Peter 5:6), and Father YAH will exalt us in due season.

As I did an overview of my 30-plus years in ministry, I found that where the church suffered the most was in the area of communication. Many times, there is a difference between what we think we have said and what a person actually heard. I find that to be true even now on my job. When an email is sent out, you can have three people read it, and they each may have a different interpretation; that's scary! I find that, when I read things over and over again, I begin to understand what the sender was trying to convey.

Two other areas of concern in connection to succession are chemistry and competency. I always taught how important it was for ministries to have people who are in proper position to operate in the gift given them of God, not of Man. Sometimes I wonder where our DNA has gone wrong when it comes to operating in the character traits of Father God. Do we really know the importance of keeping our churches strong and stable when the time comes for the baton to be passed on?

Listen, the goal of the church is key, but, more than that, there has to be a working relationship between not just Leaders but more so between members because, if it were not for them, the church couldn't thrive. When I look now at the vulnerability of the church, it behooves those still in operation to admit that, at some point, we really got it wrong and, before it's too late, we must be willing to re-evaluate and get it right. Keep in mind, too, that there will always be an absence, and that's the time you will be able to determine if cross training has been successful.

To all my sons and daughters of the cloth, please create for your ministries a life line that will survive 2024. Develop a team of Leaders that is efficient. Never be satisfied with good when you know you have been called to be great. This is a season when the church is being called to a place where you must raise the bar and stay in front of the curve. There are so many benefits to succession planning. If you are going to stay on the cutting edge, you must give more attention to improvement through the development of kingdom instruction. Church, as usual, will never foot the bill of Kingdom, so understand the importance of being ready.

No longer can you allow exhaustion to affect your excellence. Please take seriously the significant change the pandemic of 2020 made on the church, and the Pastors now trying to survive this new season. I don't know about you, but this pandemic has changed my way of thinking, as it should for those of you who know the seriousness of this time. And may the realignment of this next hour be so full of value that you come to know there must always be a vision to work towards.

Going forward, please don't get caught off guard. Put yourself in a position of being in the know, for, when you are in the know, it is this level of wisdom that has the ability to open doors. I've often said down through the years there is more to you than meets the eye, so, to those who are reading this final chapter, if you are going to discover more in this season, you must be willing to step out of the boat like Peter in the powerful chronicles of Yah's word the Bible. If you are going to be one available to preserve kingdom, you must have greater influence over the church.

YAH Father God, as in the days of Isaiah, is calling today, saying, "Who can I send, and who will go for us?" (Isaiah 6:8). Father is not just looking for people who think about the present but those who have the ability to see five to 10 years into the future. No longer can senior Leaders with a Jezebel Spirit hex others with names and titles that belittle their divine gift and calling; begin giving them the hands-on experience to better their ability to expand and grow.

Did you know that 65% of nonprofit organizations neither see the need to teach or plan for succession? Where we stand now with the church, we can't afford to be caught off guard. The church for so many years has tried to place a band-aid on vital issues or create other quick fixes, only to remain in a broken state, void of the essential Power that only comes from the Father. I declare YAH is looking now for those in the spiritual queue who are equipped and ready to bring in this next harvest of believers-in-waiting.

No longer can the church allow important issues to fall through the cracks, for the church—ever since the pandemic—is at risk of becoming extinct, by which I mean it will have no living members and will no longer be in existence. My, my, my! My Prayer for the church is that one day it will again function in the way YAH Father God ordered it in the beginning.

Let this also be a message for those that don't have a succession plan at home for their family. Fathers and Mothers, don't leave Earth with your house out of order but leave a will and instructions so your children won't have to go through issues to bury

When It's All Said and Done

you. Honor God for leaving an inheritance for even your children's children.

Another point to ponder is what can we as Leaders do to stop eating at every man's table and find out where God really wants us to serve properly. Every table (church) is not meant for consumption. Furthermore, when will the real Prophets arise, not just in word but also in deed?

If I can leave you with any lasting words of importance, it would be these:

1. Honor YAH with your heart, soul, and mind
2. Renew your relationship often, making sure you share with Him a covenant
3. Always keep Yah first in everything you do
4. Abide always in the vine (Psalm 91) who keeps you in tune
5. Let the Navigation of Heaven always be your instruction

Monica Anthony

A Word of Thanks to My Parents

Gone but never ever forgotten.
My pillars of strength who taught
me how to navigate this life in wisdom.
May my foundation always be sound
because of you
Mommy, Daddy I love you to
Infinity and beyond

www.ingramcontent.com/pod-product-compliance
Lightning Source LLC
Chambersburg PA
CBHW032302150426
43195CB00008BA/545